U-Turn and Other Poems For Christian Direction

With the Author's Reflections and Prayers
And Selected Scriptures

By Eugene Troche
Author of . . .
All Aboard! Poetry on Rails - Heaven Bound

Copyright©2010 Eugene Troche
All rights reserved.
ISBN: 1451536313
ISBN - 13: 9781451536317

To the Struggling Christian

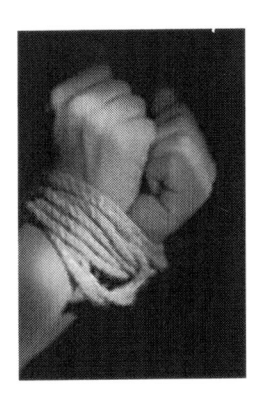

I have swept away your sins like a cloud. I have scattered your offenses like the morning mist. Oh, return to me, for I have paid the price to set you free.

Isaiah 44:22

All Scriptures in this book are quoted from:
www.biblegateway.com (NIV or NLT)

CONTENTS

I Am So Lost…	1
U-Turn	5
Trading Heaven	11
In Christ	15
The Mirror Repairer	19
Crimson Camouflage	23
Strategies of Sin	27
God's Fitting Room	31
Cruisin' Christian	35
Any Other Day	39
Behold Your God!	43
Don't Water Me Down	48
Love Genesis	52
Tune into God	56
Crafty Mr. Gotcha	60
Running into Him	65
Just Visiting	69
God's Plan of Salvation (GPS)	73
Stop the Traffic!	77
The Night Watchman	81
From the Manger…	88
To the Cross…	89
To the Empty Tomb	90
A Sliver of Christ	94
Life's Odometer	98
Holiness, the Final Frontier	102
The Finish Line – Not the End!	107

I Am So Lost...

Road signs tell drivers where they are, where they are headed, which way to turn, or, in some cases, what <u>not</u> to do. A road sign on a dry desert road can be especially helpful when one is lost. A lost traveler on such a road can stand there, wherever "there" happens to be, and do nothing, he can turn in several directions, or he can continue along the same path he was following. The traveler can also make a U-turn and retrace his tracks back, hopefully, to civilization. This book is about the "U-turns" in our lives, when we are on our own desert road, lost and spiritually dry. It is about the times that we find ourselves at the crossroads and something inside tells us that some of those roads will lead to dead-ends and disappointments, while another road, a new road, or perhaps even the very road we were once traveling on, takes us to a far better place.

Our Christian walk is no different. It is very demanding and there is no "easy button." When we reach our final destination, we will not say "oh, that was easy!" Oftentimes, however, a seemingly easier road presents itself, a road that at first sight offers enticing delicacies, pleasurable aromas, eye-pleasing images, and captivating sounds. Our attention is drawn to that road, just like a child's attention is instantly drawn to the sounds of a carnival or an ice cream truck. Our senses are captured by these wide-open roads, and these roads are wide indeed.

Jesus Christ invites us to take a different road. That road, as described in the Bible, is a narrow path with no dead-ends. At the end of that road is glory personified – Christ himself! It is only then that we will see Him clearly, as He really is. (1 John 3:2)

I am reminded of a scene in *My Cousin Vinny*, a very funny movie in which Joe Pesci, as defense attorney Gambini, cross-examines an eyewitness who testifies about what he saw through a window. Here is the exchange:

Q: Hey, Mr. Crane, what are these pictures of?

A: My house and stuff.

Q: Your house and stuff. And what is this brown stuff on the windows?

A: Dirt.

Q: Dirt? What is this rusty, dusty, dirty-looking thing over your window?

A: It's a screen.

Q: A screen? It's a screen. And what are these big things right in the middle of your view, from the middle of your window to the Sack O' Suds? What do we call these big things?

A: Trees?

Q: Trees, that's right. Don't be afraid. Just shout 'em right out when you know 'em.

Now, what are these thousands of little things that are on trees?

A: Leaves?

Q: And these bushy things between the trees?

A: Bushes?

Q: Bushes, right. So, Mr. Crane, you could positively identify the defendants for a moment of two seconds looking through this dirty window, this crud-covered screen, these trees with all these leaves on them, and I don't know how many bushes.

A: Looks like five.

Q: Ah ah, don't forget this one and this one.

A: Seven bushes.

Q: So, what do you think? Do you think it's possible you just saw two guys in a green convertible, and not necessarily these two particular guys?

A: I suppose.

Gambini: I'm finished with this guy.

I am reminded of this scene because oftentimes we think we see things clearly when in fact there are so many other things – "stuff" – in the way. Until we admit, as the eyewitness did in *My Cousin Vinny*, that perhaps we are not seeing things as clearly as we think we are, and that our view may in fact be gravely obstructed, we will never clearly see Christ in our lives or the road we should follow as Christians.

U-Turn

Turn, turn from me Lord
I have nothing to offer
How many times must I offend you?
How many times must you suffer?

I am, as the proverb goes
Like a sow that has been washed
Once again stuck in the mire
Goes about its business unabashed

Yes, I am that person
Taking your precious gifts
Grace, mercy, and love
Throwing them over the cliffs

Turn, turn from me Lord
I am not worthy of your gaze
Turn from me and leave
You must be tired of my clichés

Meaningless words that I throw at you
Empty promises are what they are
Leave me and forget me Lord
Turn from me and go afar

Those were my words to God
Though in my heart they echoed pain
I turned away and hid my face
But my true feelings I could not feign

God saw through my facade and said
From you my child I shall not turn
U-turn instead and come back to me
It is for you, my child, I yearn

U-turn and don't look back
You need me now more than ever
I shall not turn my back on you
U-turn to me, now and forever

* * *

Reflection

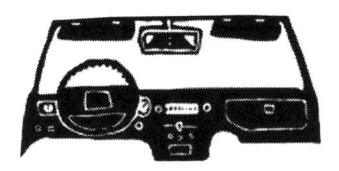

Looking Back – Moving Forward

Sometimes we feel that we have reached a point of no return. We think that this time we have really crossed the line and that there is no way that God will forgive us. True, God despises sin, but it is also true that God is abundantly merciful. God loves us and gives each individual every opportunity to make a U-turn, no matter where we are, no matter what we've done, no matter how far we've strayed. God always wants us to return to him.

The Word of God

Gauge Yourself

Jesus continued: "There was a man who had two sons. The younger one said to his father, 'Father, give me my share of the estate.' So he divided his property between them.

Not long after that, the younger son got together all he had, set off for a distant country and there squandered his wealth in wild living. After he had spent everything, there was a severe famine in that whole country, and he began to be in need. So he went and hired himself out to a citizen of that country, who sent him to his fields to feed pigs. He longed to fill his stomach with the pods that the pigs were eating, but no one gave him anything.

When he came to his senses, he said, 'How many of my father's hired men have food to spare, and here I am starving to death! I will set out and go back to my father and say to him: Father, I have sinned against heaven and against you. I am no longer worthy to be called your son; make me like one of your hired men.' So he got up and went to his father.

But while he was still a long way off, his father saw him and was filled with compassion for him; he ran to his son, threw his arms around him and kissed him."

Luke 15:11-20

Prayer

Time to Refuel!

LORD, I am so thankful for your mercy! I have turned from you and strayed so many times in my life, and yet you have always shown mercy. Instead of turning from me, you have embraced me and kissed me, celebrating my return. May I remain in that embrace and not return to my days of waste and "wild living."

LOST
CONFUSED
UNSURE
UNCLEAR
PERPLEXED
DISORIENTED
BEWILDERED

Trading Heaven

Hey, I've got a trade
Give me instant pleasure
And I'll give you heaven
Give me a million bucks
And I'll give you heaven
How about good looks and a great body
How about a small island in the Caribbean
You see, I've got this gift I can trade
It was given to me by this dude named Jesus
The fool gave it to me for nothing
That's right, nothing!
The gift is actually quite magical
You see, I've traded it before
But I somehow manage to get it back
So it's like, I can have my cake and eat it too!
I can trade the gift for some momentary pleasure
I can trade it for a passing fling
I can even trade it for cash
So, how about it?
You too can have this gift and do with it as you please
You can trade it for whatever you desire
You can trade it for whatever fancies you
Whatever, and whenever, and wherever
And to think that this fool Jesus gave it to me for nothing
An amazing and wonderful gift it is!
The way I see it, give me what I desire now
And, what's the name of that flick?
Heaven Can Wait!

* * *

Reflection

Looking Back – Moving Forward

Heaven can wait! That is oftentimes our attitude. But can it? When we play the "spiritual stock market," we cannot take it for granted that we will get up the next day and head to the trading floor, hoping to make up our losses from the day before. Tomorrow is not guaranteed. So, once we have that gift that goes by the name of *salvation*, purchased with the precious blood of Jesus Christ, we need to hold on to it for dear life. We trade it at our peril!

The Word of God

Gauge Yourself

Someone came to Jesus with this question: "Teacher, what good deed must I do to have eternal life?"

"Why ask me about what is good?" Jesus replied. "There is only One who is good. But to answer your question, if you want to receive eternal life, keep the commandments."

"Which ones?" the man asked.

And Jesus replied: "You must not murder. You must not commit adultery. You must not steal. You must not testify falsely. Honor your father and mother. Love your neighbor as yourself."

"I've obeyed all these commandments," the young man replied. "What else must I do?"

Jesus told him, "If you want to be perfect, go and sell all your possessions and give the money to the poor, and you will have treasure in heaven. Then come, follow me."

But when the young man heard this, he went away sad, for he had many possessions.

Matthew 19:16-22

Prayer

Time to Refuel!

LORD, so many of us are like the rich young man, unable to detach ourselves from the riches and the pleasures of this world, unable to make that definitive and purposeful choice of following you. There are so many things that enslave us and keep us from fully enjoying your promises. Help me so that I can break away from the things that keep me back; the things that hold me down; the things that enslave me; the things that separate me from you. I do not want to reflect the sad face of the rich young man, but the joyous and radiant face of one who says "YES!" when you ask "Who shall I send?"

In Christ

When I say that I am "In Christ"
I mean exactly that, my friend
I don't mean to say that I am "into Him"
The way I would be into some kind of trend

I am not into Him the way I'm into food
You know, "arroz con pollo" or "rice and beans"
Roast pork and ripe bananas
Not like someone would be into salad greens

I am not into Him the way I'm into music
Salsa, Merengue, R& B, Hip-Hop or Jazz
Country, Metal, or Rock
Funk, Punk or some other razzmatazz

I am not into Him the way I'm into style
The latest hair craze, the newest jeans
Expensive sneakers or the sleekest wheels
If you ask me, it's all artificial means

I am "in Christ," like the man Paul said
Not into, around, or about my Lord
In Christ is my peace and joy
In Him is my reward

In Christ!

* * *

Reflection

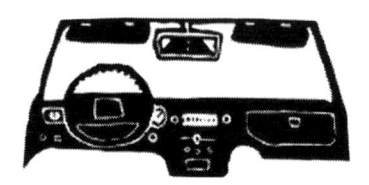

Looking Back – Moving Forward

What does it mean to be a Christian? It means to follow Christ no matter where life takes us. It means to get out of our comfort zone and not conform to this world. To be a Christian is to live "in Christ" and not be "wishy-washy" about our relationship with Him. To be a Christian is to feel Him burning within, to be driven by Him, to be ALIVE in Him!

The Word of God

Gauge Yourself

I know your deeds, that you are neither cold nor hot. I wish you were either one or the other! So, because you are lukewarm--neither hot nor cold--I am about to spit you out of my mouth. You say, "I am rich; I have acquired wealth and do not need a thing." But you do not realize that you are wretched, pitiful, poor, blind and naked.

Revelation 3:15-17

Prayer

Time to Refuel!

LORD, when I am running on empty I need to remember that it is in you that I find true peace, happiness, and freedom. But there are times when I lose this perspective and become lukewarm or even worse, again seeking comfort in the things of this world, the very same things that kept me separated from you. I pray that when I become lukewarm, the Holy Spirit may rekindle our relationship so that I may once again be alive in you.

The Mirror Repairer

Every day I look at myself
I say all is well deep in my soul
My mind is clean, my heart's at peace
My God is near, this much I know

I used to think he was not real
Or if he was, he did not care
Pain and suffering is all I saw
I hated the whole sordid affair

I looked in the mirror and saw no hope
The mirror was broken, reflecting my life
Each crack a scar, each crack a tare
The image of a person so full of strife

But when that mirror was almost shattered
And my life so broken, my scars so deep
Jesus Christ, the repairer of souls
Healed and restored me, another lost sheep

He repaired my life, my broken body
With my hope renewed, my scars were gone
I now look into a brand new mirror
Repaired and restored by Christ the Son

* * *

Reflection

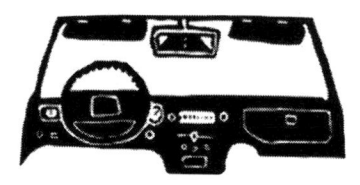

Looking Back – Moving Forward

Many in this world walk around with broken hearts, broken bodies, and shattered hopes. Life has not been kind and the future, well, what future? When we feel this way, there is no man-made medicine to cure us. When we feel this way, what we need is to turn to Jesus Christ. Jesus heals the broken-hearted and restores hope to the hopeless. That is the truth that lifts us from a state of despair to a state of grace and peace. That is the truth that sets us free!

The Word of God

Gauge Yourself

And the God of all grace, who called you to his eternal glory in Christ, after you have suffered a little while, will himself restore you and make you strong, firm and steadfast.

1 Peter 5:10

This means that anyone who belongs to Christ has become a new person. The old life is gone; a new life has begun!

2 Corinthians 5:17

And you will know the truth, and the truth will set you free.

John 8:32

Prayer

Time to Refuel!

LORD, I know that being a Christian does not mean that I will be free of difficulties, free of suffering. But I would rather go through those times with you than without you. You are my strength and my fortress. It is in you that I find restoration and peace. It is in you that I am truly free.

Crimson Camouflage

Cover me with the blood of the Lamb
Keep me hidden from the evil one
Frustrate his purposes in me, my God
And fulfill the promises of Christ your Son

Camouflage me with your blood, my Lord
The blood you shed for me on the cross
Blood from your hands, your feet, your head
Blood from your side, shed for my cause

The blood that sanctifies, blood that gives hope
Blood that cleanses, blood that atones
The blood of the Lamb that was shed for all
The blood of the man with no broken bones

Oh, Crimson Camouflage, cover me from head to toe
Seal me tight until the day my Savior comes again
Camouflage every cell, every hair, my very soul
With the blood of the One on Calvary slain

* * *

Reflection

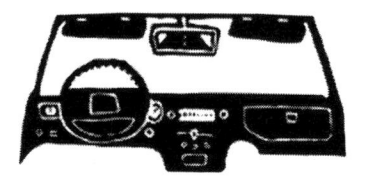

Looking Back – Moving Forward

We pray that God may keep us from all evil. The truth is, however, that sin is all around us and temptations are perennial. As Christians, we need to be prepared to do battle, day in and day out, because the battles will come. But although we are at times exposed, God provides us with the means to victory.

The Word of God

Gauge Yourself

Psalm 3:3 But you, O Lord, are a shield around me; you are my glory, the one who holds my head high.

Psalm 5:12 For you bless the godly, O Lord; you surround them with your shield of love.

Psalm 18:2 The Lord is my rock, my fortress, and my savior; my God is my rock, in whom I find protection. He is my shield, the power that saves me, and my place of safety.

Psalm 18:30 God's way is perfect. All the Lord's promises prove true. He is a shield for all who look to him for protection.

Prayer

Time to Refuel!

Yes, LORD, in you I find the strength and courage to face all difficulties and temptations, and to pursue the path you have set before me. I understand that, because of the human condition, the road is hard, full of stumbling stones, hairpin turns, and pitfalls. But with you, LORD, I will not lose hope.

Strategies of Sin

Loopholes in the heart
Loopholes in the soul
The strategies of sin
Barriers to becoming whole

The mind against the heart
The heart against the soul
The strategies of sin
Obstacles to the ultimate goal

The left hand doesn't know
What the right hand is doing
The strategies of sin
This stuff keeps on brewing

Tomorrow will be different
Tomorrow I will change
The strategies of sin
Tomorrow never came

None of it matters
There is no heaven or hell
The strategies of sin
That's how mankind fell

* * *

Reflection

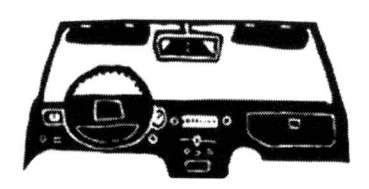

Looking Back – Moving Forward

What does it all matter? Despite our God-given free will, we cannot "will" heaven or hell away. John Lennon sang:

> *Imagine there's no heaven*
> *It's easy if you try*
> *No hell below us*
> *Above us only sky*

The truth is, there <u>are</u> evil forces at work in this world and the strategies of sin are indeed powerful. But more powerful is our God – we just don't always see it. There is a little book titled <u>Your God is Too Small</u> by J.B. Phillips. That, in a nutshell, is why we oftentimes fall prey to the strategies of sin. Think BIG, my friend, because God is BIG!

The Word of God

Gauge Yourself

Now the serpent was more crafty than any of the wild animals the LORD God had made. He said to the woman, "Did God really say, 'You must not eat from any tree in the garden'?"

The woman said to the serpent, "We may eat fruit from the trees in the garden, but God did say, 'You must not eat fruit from the tree that is in the middle of the garden, and you must not touch it, or you will die.' "

"You will not surely die," the serpent said to the woman. "For God knows that when you eat of it your eyes will be opened, and you will be like God, knowing good and evil."

When the woman saw that the fruit of the tree was good for food and pleasing to the eye, and also desirable for gaining wisdom, she took some and ate it. She also gave some to her husband, who was with her, and he ate it. Then the eyes of both of them were opened, and they realized they were naked; so they sewed fig leaves together and made coverings for themselves.

Genesis 3:1-7

Prayer

Time to Refuel!

LORD, you have provided me with the best defense against the strategies of sin – your word. I pray that your word may continue to give me life and strength, courage and hope. Although my best strategy is to stay out of the serpent's lair, I know that there are times when I must do battle from within that lair. It is then that I truly need to trust in you.

God's Fitting Room

Come into God's fitting room
And try his wardrobe on for size
You go in looking and feeling one way
But come out with a new look in your eyes

A new you, a changed person
No way will you not change in there
A whole new outlook on life you'll have
Come in and see for yourself, if you dare

Come in with your dirty rags, or your rich adorn
Bring your garb and your bling bling too
Throw it all into God's fitting room
Where you'll find all things become new

Go in weak and powerless, and come out strong
Put on the belt of truth and the helmet of salvation
Hold on to the shield of faith and the sword of the Spirit
Accept no "knock-offs," there is no imitation

In God's fitting room you'll find all you need
To fight the good fight and run the good race
So enter and put on the full armor of God
And the devil himself will never keep pace

* * *

Reflection

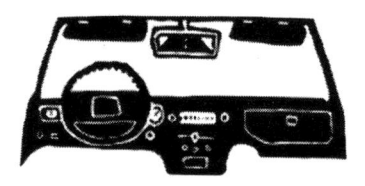

Looking Back – Moving Forward

When we wake up every morning, we should consider more than what shirt or blouse to wear or what tie would go best with a particular suit. We should ask ourselves whether we are properly attired to meet the day's spiritual challenges. And if the answer is no, then we need to ask God to clothe us with His heavenly attire. And, don't worry, He knows your size.

The Word of God

Gauge Yourself

Finally, be strong in the Lord and in his mighty power. Put on the full armor of God so that you can take your stand against the devil's schemes. For our struggle is not against flesh and blood, but against the rulers, against the authorities, against the powers of this dark world and against the spiritual forces of evil in the heavenly realms. Therefore put on the full armor of God, so that when the day of evil comes, you may be able to stand your ground, and after you have done everything, to stand. Stand firm then, with the belt of truth buckled around your waist, with the breastplate of righteousness in place, and with your feet fitted with the readiness that comes from the gospel of peace. In addition to all this, take up the shield of faith, with which you can extinguish all the flaming arrows of the evil one. Take the helmet of salvation and the sword of the Spirit, which is the word of God.

Ephesians 6:10-17

Prayer

Time to Refuel!

LORD, I know that there are battles to be fought every day and that what I need more than brand name clothing is the spiritual armor described in <u>Ephesians</u>. Properly dressed, I can, like David, fight giants, those that are seen and those that are not seen.

Cruisin' Christian

Driving down the highway
I look to my left and I look to my right
I see heads bopping and hands waving
The lips are moving from daybreak to night

People are cruisin' to their music
Pop, R&B, rock, metal and jazz
Snapping their fingers and hitting the dash
Grooving to the music with a lot of pizzazz

Some of that music is cool with me too
But I must admit the hard stuff's too much
A little light music, a Latin ballad will do
A little jazz, o yeah, that's a nice touch

But my favorite music of all heard on the dial
Is the music that worships and praises Christ the Son
That old Christian tune still holding its own
The contemporary Christian beat that hits a home run

I'm a Cruisin' Christian, that's what I am
Bopping my head as I work on the clutch
I snap my fingers and beat on the dash
In the name of the Lord, whom I love very much

I'm a Cruisin' Christian on the highways of life
My lips move to the beat of TobyMac and 4Him
I move and I groove to Velasquez and Camp
Cruisin' to Worship and Praise, a Cruisin' Christian I am

* * *

Reflection

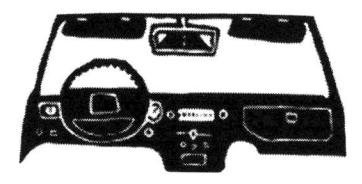

Looking Back – Moving Forward

They say that music calms the savage beast; that it can lift up the soul and heal broken hearts. Music, joyful lyrics or sad, has always been a beautiful way to praise the LORD. So, hit the high note, or low, sing in tune, or out, and let your voice sing with joy. Angels themselves will lift up every note to heaven.

The Word of God

Gauge Yourself

Psalm 33:3 Sing to him a new song; play skillfully, and shout for joy.

Psalm 96:1 Sing to the LORD a new song; sing to the LORD, all the earth.

Psalm 98:1 Sing a new song to the LORD, for he has done wonderful deeds. His right hand has won a mighty victory; his holy arm has shown his saving power!

Psalm 144:9 I will sing a new song to you, O God; on the ten-stringed lyre I will make music to you.

Prayer

Time to Refuel!

LORD, there are all types of music in the world. The Bible talks about singing psalms, hymns, and spiritual songs to worship you. (Ephesians 5:19) Music is a wonderful way to praise you and to come together in prayer. I pray that every day notes of joyful praise rise up from my heart to your throne in heaven.

Any Other Day

Any other day
I would have cursed that person out
Pocketed that money
Bought that dirty magazine
Snorted that drug
Or pulled the trigger
But not today
Today is different
Today I am a different person
I am a new person in Christ
Today is not like any other day
And tomorrow will never be the same
Tomorrow, I will not look back
For tomorrow holds a promise
Every tomorrow holds a promise
A promise of eternal joy
A promise of eternal peace
A promise that my change today
Will not be in vain come tomorrow
Any other day, but not today
For today I am His!

* * *

Reflection

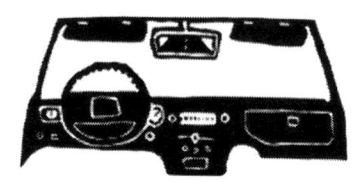

Looking Back – Moving Forward

Lyrics from Stephen Curtis Chapman's "The Change":

Well I got myself a T-shirt that says what I believe
I got letters on my bracelet to serve as my ID
I got the necklace and the key chain
And almost everything a good Christian needs, yeah

I got the little Bible magnets on my refrigerator door
And a welcome mat to bless you
Before you walk across my floor
I got a Jesus bumper sticker
And the outline of a fish stuck on my car
And even though this stuff's all well and good, yeah
I cannot help but ask myself—

What about the change?
What about the difference?

The Word of God

Gauge Yourself

Therefore, if anyone is in Christ, he is a new creation; the old has gone, the new has come!

2 Corinthians 5:17

Neither do men pour new wine into old wineskins. If they do, the skins will burst, the wine will run out and the wineskins will be ruined. No, they pour new wine into new wineskins, and both are preserved.

Mathew 9:17

Prayer

Time to Refuel!

So many times, LORD, I find myself in the same old rut. I change, but only momentarily. I feel like a new person, but only for a time. I want so much to feel like that new wineskin, to be that "new creation" Paul talks about; to experience that profound change that only Christ can bring. And, yes, I want that change to last forever.

Behold Your God!

How many of us really understand
What it means to behold our God
To behold His power and majesty
To behold all He has made
And all He has done
To behold with awesome wonder
All that is His creation
Instead, we marvel at our own selves
At our own abilities, talents and ingenuity
We praise each other for our accomplishments
We take delight in our inventions and discoveries
We look and smile, pleased and proud
But when you find yourself alone
At the very top of some mountain, as I have
Looking around and seeing His handiwork
Hills, valleys, rivers and trees
While hearing the voices of nature
And, yes, an occasional church bell or two
When you are up there alone
And you feel an incredible sense of peace
You cannot help but wonder about God
You cannot help but behold His glorious splendor
Behold His mighty spirit and majestic presence
Behold the awesome wonder that is His creation
You cannot help but sing praises to Him
For you have beheld your God
Even if only for a brief moment
Cherish it and hope for another
Behold your Creator
Behold your God!

* * *

Reflection

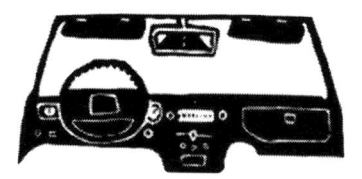

Looking Back – Moving Forward

Somewhere on a mountain in northern New Jersey is a bench with the inscription *Behold Your God* carved into the wood. If you sit on that bench and look around, you will better understand the previous poem. But, of course, you need not come to New Jersey to do that. LOL! You can do it wherever you are. True, what many around the world see is not so pretty. There is poverty, abuse, war, pollution, broken homes, etc. But the day that we stop seeing God in the world will be the day we lose all hope.

The Word of God

Gauge Yourself

Then the LORD answered Job from the whirlwind:
"Who is this that questions my wisdom
with such ignorant words?
Brace yourself like a man,
because I have some questions for you,
and you must answer them.

"Where were you when I laid the foundations of the earth?
Tell me, if you know so much.
Who determined its dimensions
and stretched out the surveying line?
What supports its foundations,
and who laid its cornerstone
as the morning stars sang together
and all the angels shouted for joy?

"Who kept the sea inside its boundaries
as it burst from the womb,
and as I clothed it with clouds
and wrapped it in thick darkness?

For I locked it behind barred gates,
limiting its shores.
I said, 'This far and no farther will you come.
Here your proud waves must stop!'

Job 38:1-11

Prayer

Time to Refuel!

There are times when we, like Job, question the way the world turns. We wonder why there is so much strife and grief. But although at times it may be hard to see, the bottom line is and always has been that God is in control. To use a military phrase, God has the "con." Although at times things seem so out of place, all things will one day be restored. It is this truth that we must put our trust in. It is this truth that refuels our faith.

Don't Water Me Down

Don't' water me down
I am strong and powerful
But also humble and tender
I am full of love and compassion
Though sometimes stern and demanding

Don't water me down
I am caring and forgiving
But I can judge both you and your brother
I am never off key and always on point
Though I have been frequently misunderstood

Don't water me down
I have been around from the beginning of time
But time as you know it will end, while I will go on
I have been proclaimed by the rich and the poor
Though I have also been rejected by many

Don't water me down
I am the way, the truth and the life
I am the one true hope for all of mankind
I am the answer to life's many problems
I AM the Word of God

* * *

Reflection

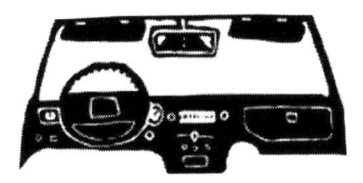

Looking Back – Moving Forward

Webster's dictionary defines "watered down" as follows: "to reduce or temper the force or effectiveness of." The Word of God is oftentimes diluted or watered down and as such it tends to lose its "force and effectiveness." It is like drinking a watered down cup of coffee – it just doesn't have the same "kick." But just like we sometimes need a strong cup of coffee, we need to hear the Word of God the way it was meant to be heard. If I was asked to suggest an eleventh commandment, I would humbly state it thus: "**Thou shall not water down my word.**"

The Word of God

Gauge Yourself

We reject all shameful deeds and underhanded methods. We don't try to trick anyone or distort the word of God. We tell the truth before God, and all who are honest know this.

2 Corinthians 4:2

For the word of God is alive and powerful. It is sharper than the sharpest two-edged sword, cutting between soul and spirit, between joint and marrow. It exposes our innermost thoughts and desires.

Hebrews 4:12

Prayer

Time to Refuel!

LORD, I know that your word is powerful and true. When I read your word, I am challenged and at the same time comforted. In truth, your word exposes who I am and guides me to the place where I need to be. Thank you God for the road map you have so graciously given to us in your Word.

Love Genesis

Everything was fine, or at least it all seemed fine
Anyone looking in from the outside would think
What a perfect and beautiful family they make
With no problems, no conflict, not even a kink

And perhaps it was that way one day
But that day seems to be now long gone
No longer can we mask and fake it
The joy, the smiles, and even the fun

Each day now appears to be a struggle
The peace and the trust have all broken down
Communications are strained and so are our vocal chords
The smile turned upside down, so it looks like a frown

But is it all gone, can it be retrieved
Gathered anew, brought back from the dead
Can it all be restored, refreshed in our hearts
Or is it too late, nothing left, not even a shred

I'm a Christian, so I believe there is hope
All we need is to find what started it all
We need to go back to the family seed
I think it was love, that's what I recall

So let's renew our hearts, go back to square one
Remove all that stands in our way
Let us seek God, the expert on love
For he laid true love in a manger one day

* * *

Reflection

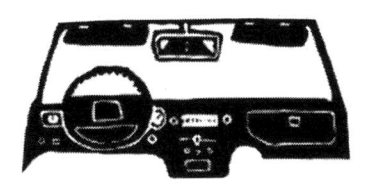

Looking Back – Moving Forward

Does it all come down to love? Let's take a look at another song by Steven Curtis Chapman, "All About Love":

> *We've got CDs, tapes and videos,*
> *radios and TV shows*
> *Conferences, retreats and seminars*
> *We've got books and magazines to read*
> *on everything from A to Z*
> *And a web to surf from anywhere we are*
> *But I hope with all this information*
> *buzzing through our brains*
> *That we will not let our hearts forget*
> *the most important thing is*
>
> *Love love love love love …it's all about*
> *Love love love love love*
> *Everything else comes down to this*
> *Nothing any higher on the list than love*
> *It's all about love*

The Word of God

Gauge Yourself

If I speak in the tongues of men and of angels, but have not love, I am only a resounding gong or a clanging cymbal. If I have the gift of prophecy and can fathom all mysteries and all knowledge, and if I have a faith that can move mountains, but have not love, I am nothing. If I give all I possess to the poor and surrender my body to the flames, but have not love, I gain nothing.

1 Corinthians 13:1-3

For God so loved the world that he gave his one and only Son, that whoever believes in him shall not perish but have eternal life.

John 3:16

Prayer

Time to Refuel!
(Write your own prayer here)

Tune into God

Ask yourself, what are you tuning into?
What is that signal that you are honing in on?
What is that message that's grabbing your attention?
What is the latest enticing sound you've come upon?

Ask yourself, where does it all take you?
How has your life improved, what gain is there?
Tuning into this and tuning into that
Surfing for whatever is on the air

Next time you reach for the dial, tune into God
God loves you and desires your heart, mind and soul
He wants you to tune into Him in worship and prayer
Don't tune Him out, He'll make you whole

Once you're tuned into God, you'll understand
No other place on the dial is worth tuning into
So, once set to God, don't touch that dial
His love is real and his promises are true

When you tune into God, you tune into love
His message is joy and peace, his message is pure
To fine-tune it all, he sent Christ his Son
And through the Holy Spirit his signal will endure

* * *

Reflection

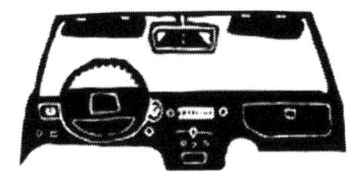

Looking Back – Moving Forward

There are so many times that we reach over, change the dial of life, and tune away from God. What we need to remember is that Christ is the tower that keeps us tuned into God. So, whenever we lose the signal, we need to look for the tower in the shape of a cross. In no time at all we will once again be tuned into God. Try it, it works!

The Word of God

Gauge Yourself

O Lord, do good to those who are good, whose hearts are in tune with you.

Psalm 125:4

Tune your ears to wisdom, and concentrate on understanding.

Proverbs 2:2

Set your minds on things above, not on earthly things.

Colossians 3:2

Prayer

Time to Refuel!

LORD, the airwaves of life are quite congested these days. There is so much that we can tune into. But I want to be in tune with you. I want to stay focused on those things that spiritually enrich my life and the lives of those around me. I want to set my mind on things above. But I realize there are times when I lose your signal. When that happens, help me find the tower in the shape of a cross so that I can get back in tune with you.

Crafty Mr. Gotcha

Here I am, again, my friend
We have met once or twice
Or need I reintroduce myself?
I'm Mr. Gotcha - that should suffice

You try to ignore me, even forget me
And you manage to do so, for a time
But when you think you've lost me
I say "gotcha," this time you're mine

My job is to break through the good in you
Sometimes it takes less effort, sometimes more
But as certain as the sun rises and the moon shines
I'm real and I'm here, not some made-up folklore

When you think you're safe and secure
I trip you up and make you fall
Even if only for a moment or two
I can say "gotcha," you've answered my call

Sometimes I need to work hard, sometimes I don't
But I always find a way to get your attention
Though usually in dark places, and when you're alone
I can also say "gotcha" anywhere in creation

So, look for me, or not, I will find you
Anytime you drop your guard, I'm there for sure
My only problem is when your faith in Him is strong
In that case I lose, no matter what I conjure

I'll go on to another, and say "gotcha" to him
As for you, I'll pass and return another season
So long as He is in you, I cannot prevail
But I can always come back, just give me a reason

* * *

Reflection

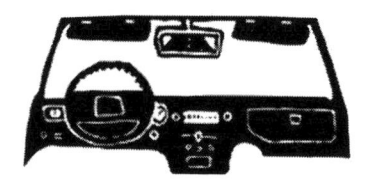

Looking Back – Moving Forward

Satan is not the "boogeyman" or some mythical three-headed creature. Satan is not a Hollywood "dark force" of some kind. His craftiness and deceit are real forces we have to contend with. He will hang around as long as we let him. He will wait, watch, and seize any opening, no matter how slight. We must be strong in the LORD so that Satan's craftiness does not take hold and prevail.

The Word of God

Gauge Yourself

Then Jesus was led by the Spirit into the desert to be tempted by the devil. After fasting forty days and forty nights, he was hungry. The tempter came to him and said, "If you are the Son of God, tell these stones to become bread."

Jesus answered, "It is written: 'Man does not live on bread alone, but on every word that comes from the mouth of God.'"

Matthew 4:1-10

Stay alert! Watch out for your great enemy, the devil. He prowls around like a roaring lion, looking for someone to devour. Stand firm against him, and be strong in your faith. Remember that your Christian brothers and sisters all over the world are going through the same kind of suffering you are.

1 Peter 5:8-9

Prayer

Time to Refuel!

I pray in the name of Jesus Christ that I remain alert and watchful and that I reject Satan's trappings. I pray that I may not be ensnared by his crafty trickery and his empty promises. I pray for strength to resist his temptations, like Jesus did in the desert.

Running into Him

Spiritually dry, dwindling faith
Doubting your salvation today?
You're focusing on your troubles too much
Instead you should go and pray

But who am I to tell you that?
I'm just someone you happen to run into
A stranger or perhaps an old friend
Or just someone who ran into you

Strangers running into strangers
Old friends running into each other
At a corner drugstore or at the supermarket
Perhaps someone that calls you "brother"

Or perhaps it was Jesus you ran into
But you did not see it at the time
All you saw was a stranger
Asking if you could spare a dime

* * *

Reflection

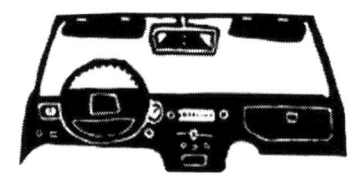

Looking Back – Moving Forward

Oftentimes we run into people and we think it a mere coincidence. Ninety-nine times out of a hundred it is. But sometimes that person was put in our path by God for a reason. We just need to figure out the reason.

The Word of God

Gauge Yourself

That same day two of Jesus' followers were walking to the village of Emmaus, seven miles from Jerusalem. As they walked along they were talking about everything that had happened. As they talked and discussed these things, Jesus himself suddenly came and began walking with them. But God kept them from recognizing him...By this time they were nearing Emmaus and the end of their journey. Jesus acted as if he were going on, but they begged him, "Stay the night with us, since it is getting late." So he went home with them. As they sat down to eat, he took the bread and blessed it. Then he broke it and gave it to them. Suddenly, their eyes were opened, and they recognized him. And at that moment he disappeared!

They said to each other, "Didn't our hearts burn within us as he talked with us on the road and explained the Scriptures to us?"

Luke 24:13-32

Prayer

Time to Refuel!

LORD, my prayer is simple: I pray that I may not miss your presence, anywhere, anytime, but that I may celebrate it and give thanks. Amen.

Just Visiting

I'm a visitor, this is not my home
My stay is but a whisper
In the expanse of space and time
My body is but a vessel, a channel
To carry out God's work
To love and to serve Him
To say here I am, send me
I do not live for the today and the now
My tomorrows come and go
My SOUL purpose is eternal
My time on earth will one day pass
This flesh and blood is but a tent
At times weathered and beaten
Tattered and leaking
But that's O.K., for it is only temporary
From dust it came and to dust it shall return
For I'm just visiting, this is not my home

* * *

Reflection

Looking Back – Moving Forward

"Here today and gone tomorrow," a cliché, but nevertheless true. The funeral of a child always brings this home; natural disasters around the world always brings this home; soldiers dying abroad always brings this home; AIDS always brings this home. "Here today and gone tomorrow," just a cliché?

The Word of God

Gauge Yourself

For we know that when this earthly tent we live in is taken down (that is, when we die and leave this earthly body), we will have a house in heaven, an eternal body made for us by God himself and not by human hands. We grow weary in our present bodies, and we long to put on our heavenly bodies like new clothing.

2 Corinthians 5:1-2

"Lord, remind me how brief my time on earth will be. Remind me that my days are numbered – how fleeting my life is. You have made my life no longer than the width of my hand. My entire lifetime is just a moment to you; at best, each of us is but a breath."

We are merely moving shadows, and all our busy rushing ends in nothing. We heap up wealth, not knowing who will spend it.

Psalm 39:4-6

Hear my prayer, O LORD! Listen to my cries for help! Don't ignore my tears. For I am your guest – a traveler passing through, as my ancestors were before me.

Psalm 39:12

Prayer

Time to Refuel!

LORD, I know I am a visitor here, but visitors can also leave their mark. This may not be my permanent home, but it is, for a time, whatever I make of it. I want to give more and take less; work diligently at whatever I do; raise my children as best I could; lend a hand or two to those in need; and, no matter what, always serve you.

God's Plan of Salvation (GPS)

Our ancestors used the stars, sun, and moon
To find their way and not get lost
Nature provided the means
At very little or no cost

Today we have quite a gadget
The Global Positioning System or GPS
Created for the military at first
But now enjoying popular success

A complicated thing this GPS
Involving multiple satellites and receivers
You could get your own in a vehicle or handheld
Some are for experts and some for beginners

But I want to share with you a different GPS
One that will help you find your way
No matter how lost you are or for how long
So you don't lose hope, so you don't dismay

God's Plan of Salvation is that GPS
It will guide you from morn till night
Our hearts and minds serve as receivers
And Jesus Christ is our satellite

Once lost, now found
God's Plan of Salvation
The best GPS you'll ever need
No better GPS in all creation

* * *

Reflection

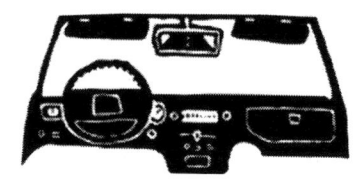

Looking Back – Moving Forward

GPS devices are marvelous things! Technology continues to gain speed and it moves so fast it is hard for us to keep up with it. We purchase something today and tomorrow it is obsolete! Well, God's Plan of Salvation has been around for a long, long time, and it will never go obsolete. And while others have tried to improve on it, it just isn't possible!

The Word of God

Gauge Yourself

Christ was sacrificed once to take away the sins of many people; and he will appear a second time, not to bear sin, but to bring salvation to those who are waiting for him.

Hebrews 9:28

For if the message spoken by angels was binding, and every violation and disobedience received its just punishment, how shall we escape if we ignore such a great salvation? This salvation, which was first announced by the Lord, was confirmed to us by those who heard him. God also testified to it by signs, wonders and various miracles, and gifts of the Holy Spirit distributed according to his will.

Hebrews 2:2-4

Prayer

Time to Refuel!

Oh LORD, your plan of salvation is perfect. You laid it in a manger for all of humanity to see. You have continuously provided us with "signs, wonders, and various miracles" so that we do not lose our way. Oh, how can we ignore it? How and at what price?

Stop the Traffic!

Coming to a traffic light one day
I saw that man again
The one with the sign that read
Brother, could you spare some change

I put my hand in my pocket
Pulled out a dollar or two
But noticed the cars behind me
And the van in my rear view

And as the light turned green
I could not stop as planned
Not wanting to stop the traffic, I moved
Past the man with the outstretched hand

Then I thought to myself
I should have stopped for the man
I should have stopped the traffic
And not worry about the man in the van

I should have stopped the traffic
And reached out to the poor man's hand
I should have stopped the traffic
Even if the man behind didn't understand

* * *

Reflection

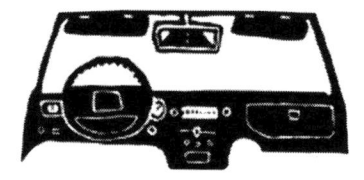

Looking Back – Moving Forward

Sometimes in order not to annoy or inconvenience others we pass up opportunities to help someone in need. Instead, we move on and look away, making believe we never saw the outstretched hand. We might even say a prayer and have faith that someone else will provide, not seeing that perhaps it was our responsibility, not someone else's.

The Word of God

Gauge Yourself

What good is it, my brothers, if a man claims to have faith but has no deeds? Can such faith save him? Suppose a brother or sister is without clothes and daily food. If one of you says to him, "Go, I wish you well; keep warm and well fed," but does nothing about his physical needs, what good is it?

James 2:14-16

One man gives freely, yet gains even more; another withholds unduly, but comes to poverty.

A generous man will prosper; he who refreshes others will himself be refreshed.

Proverbs 11:24-25

Prayer

Time to Refuel!
[Write your own prayer here]

The Night Watchman

Deafening noises surrounded me
I was blinded by all the "bling-bling"
I couldn't see past tomorrow
And who knew what the next day would bring

I heard talk about some god
I didn't see him, I didn't hear him
But others said they did
I thought it was just their whim

It's a crutch, I would say
I didn't need this god of theirs
Prayer, worship and going to church?
I always thought that stuff was for squares

Nothing in my life told me otherwise
My parents broke up when I was five
I was a punching bag for the local bully
I did what I could just to survive

But then one day I met this god
I was alone in a cell in some county jail
I spent the night with the night watch guard
Some blind old man who could only read Braille

I said to myself, how dumb is that!
A blind old man guarding the cell
All he cared about was reading his Bible
And preaching to me about heaven and hell

I told the man I knew all about hell
Why, I was an expert on that subject
I shared with him my sad and sorry story
How nothing but grief did I expect

The old man listened to me like no one had
His wrinkled face strangely peaceful
And with his old bony fingers across each page
The blind man read to me from the Bible

All night long the old man shared the story of God
Of his love and mercy, and of Christ his Son
To my surprise, I found myself listening intently
And wished that the old man was never done

But morning came and the old man left
And at the table sat the morning guard
He picked up the Bible and began to read
Though he did not have for it the same regard

After some time he put the book down
And I asked if I could borrow the Bible
He laughed out loud and asked
You mean this old jailhouse manual?

I told him of how I had spent the night
With the old blind guard reading the Bible
The guard once again laughed out loud
As he put the book down on the table

He said there could be no blind old man
Because there was no guard on watch that night
He explained that the jail was short-handed
Because the jailhouse budget was very tight

So it was that night that I first met God
And learned about his love for me
Now I understand and I believe
Because in that cell, God set me free

* * *

Reflection

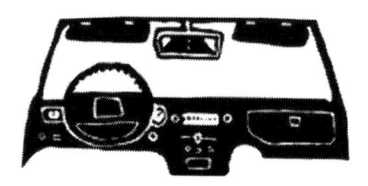

Looking Back – Moving Forward

There are many stories of people "finding" God in prison. I don't doubt that. Paul himself, as did a number of other followers of Christ, spent much time in prison. In fact, Paul himself put many in prison before his conversion. Even today, Christians are incarcerated for expressing their faith. So, actually, it would not be unusual for someone in prison to encounter God, considering that some of his best ambassadors have been there too.

The Word of God

Gauge Yourself

I have worked much harder, been in prison more frequently, been flogged more severely, and been exposed to death again and again.

2 Corinthians 11:23

About midnight Paul and Silas were praying and singing hymns to God, and the other prisoners were listening to them. Suddenly there was such a violent earthquake that the foundations of the prison were shaken. At once all the prison doors flew open, and everybody's chains came loose.

Acts 16:25-26

Do not be afraid of what you are about to suffer. I tell you, the devil will put some of you in prison to test you, and you will suffer persecution for ten days. Be faithful, even to the point of death, and I will give you the crown of life.

Revelation 2:10

Prayer

Time to Refuel!

LORD, I understand that prisons come in many shapes and forms, and that not all prisons have four walls and a barred door. The Bible talks about being a "prisoner of sin," but it also talks about being a "prisoner of Christ." I pray that you break the shackles that have been keeping me a prisoner of my own sins and that I instead become a prisoner of Christ, just like Paul and Silas.

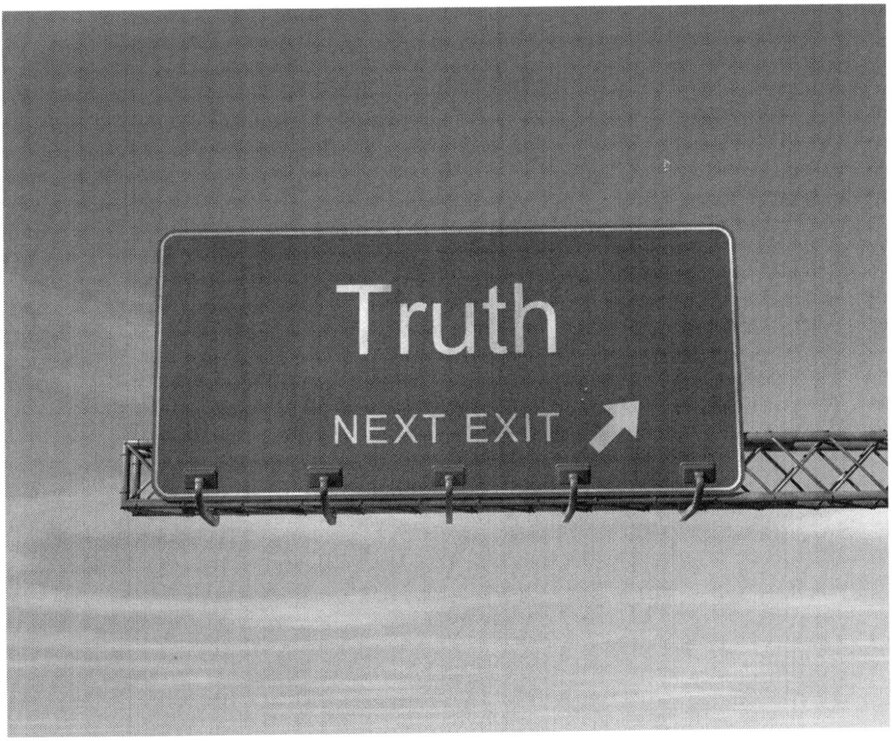
Truth
NEXT EXIT

From the Manger . . .

Come out of the manger, you say
You want me to claim my royal throne
To leave this stable and have the world worship me
To accept my place as the King of Kings

I say to you, leave your place among women and men
Come into this manger and see what I see, feel what I feel
Would a king be born in a stable?
In a strange land, among oxen and sheep?

You speak to me about a throne, I had a heavenly throne
You speak of royal garb, I left that all behind
I traded Heaven's glorious light
For the darkness of my mother Mary's womb

I don't know that I want to get out of this manger
I think I want to go back to the womb, to feel safe and secure
Once I climb out of this manger and into the world
The path I must take, I fear, will be a difficult one

Perhaps I'll stay in this manger, I'm afraid of what lies ahead
The road appears too hard and I'm not sure I'll be strong enough
Perhaps, I'll just stay in this manger and never grow up
Perhaps, I'll just lay here and never come out

* * *

To the Cross . . .

Come down, come down from that cross, you say
You want me to come down and put on my kingly robe
Leave this cross, these nails and this pain, you say
You wish for me to come down and take my seat at the throne

I say to you, again, leave your place among women and men
Climb onto this cross and see what I see, feel what I feel
Experience what it's like to hang on a cross
To be nailed here and there, to be hung among thieves

Thirty-three years ago you asked me to climb out of my manger
I told you how afraid I was, I was just a baby, you see
But then, a star brightened the sky and melted my fears away
A heavenly voice said, come out, there is work to be done

So I got out of my manger and followed the path set by my Father
Along the way, I met many a soul that had lost their way home
I realized then, I had to bring the sheep back to the fold
To reconcile God and man, that was my task, as was foretold

Does the manger make sense from up here on the cross?
Do I now understand, in spite of the pain, the why of my birth?
You've followed me from the manger to this cross
Perhaps you can explain, tell me there's more

* * *

To the Empty Tomb

Come out, come out of that man-made tomb, you say
You want me to come out and take my revenge
To call on heavenly armies and slay those who put me here
To cut short my stay in this tomb, to rise and strike back

I say to you, yet again, leave your place among women and men
Come into this tomb and see what I see, feel what I feel
Darker than dark and more silent than the softest of whispers
Abandoned even by my closest friends, whom I trusted and loved

Thirty-three years ago you asked me to climb out of my manger
I climbed out at my heavenly Father's behest, to fulfill His word
I followed His plan, from the manger, to the cross, to this tomb
His every command I honored, every detail, no matter the cost

Just yesterday, you pleaded for me to climb down from the cross
To escape from the very jaws of death, and turn my back on my Father
I turned a deaf ear to your pleas, rejecting this one last temptation
Embracing my Father's will, accepting what was foretold

To die on the cross, for your sins and the sins of the world
To bridge the abyss between God and man, that was my task
The manger, the cross, and tomorrow the empty tomb
I now finally understand, that was my Father's ultimate plan

* * *

Reflection

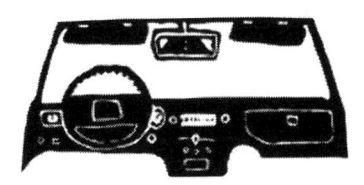

Looking Back – Moving Forward

Radio Shack's advertising slogan is "you've got questions, we've got answers." Truth is, everyone is looking for answers. In today's web-based world, answers to questions come a lot more quickly than they used to. There appears to be a website for everything and anything. For example, people go to doctors with a diagnosis in hand claiming that all they need is a prescription. Here is a suggestion: Follow the "link" from the manger, to the cross, to the empty tomb, and you will find more than answers, you will find hope and peace.

The Word of God

Gauge Yourself

Early on Sunday morning, as the new day was dawning, Mary Magdalene and the other Mary went out to visit the tomb.

Suddenly there was a great earthquake! For an angel of the Lord came down from heaven, rolled aside the stone, and sat on it. His face shone like lightning, and his clothing was as white as snow. The guards shook with fear when they saw him, and they fell into a dead faint.

Then the angel spoke to the women. "Don't be afraid!" he said. "I know you are looking for Jesus, who was crucified. He isn't here! He is risen from the dead, just as he said would happen. Come, see where his body was lying. And now, go quickly and tell his disciples that he has risen from the dead, and he is going ahead of you to Galilee. You will see him there. Remember what I have told you."

Matthew 28:1-7

Prayer

Time to Refuel!

My God, my God, thank you for the manger, for the cross, and most importantly for the empty tomb. It is the empty tomb that gives us Hope! He is risen! Alleluia! Alleluia! He is risen!

A Sliver of Christ

If I could be a sliver of Christ
A slim barely noticeable sliver
If I could convey a sliver of his love
However small it may appear
If I could imitate a sliver of his charity
A sliver of Christ I would be

If I could but offer a sliver of his friendship
Narrow as it might seem
If I could exhibit a sliver of his compassion
Though barely visible to the naked eye
If I could model a sliver of his kindness
A sliver of Christ I would be

If I could demonstrate a sliver of his obedience
No matter how slight it may seem
If I could but show a sliver of his mercy
No matter how limited that may be
If I could reveal a sliver of his glory to others
A sliver of Christ I would be

If I could exemplify a sliver of his humility
No matter how minute such may be
If I could bring to light a sliver of his humanity
For the rest of humanity to see
If I could touch upon a sliver of his divinity
A sliver of Christ I would be

If I could but a sliver be
A sliver of Christ I would be

* * *

Reflection

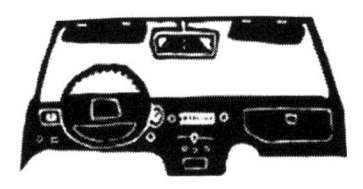

Looking Back – Moving Forward

Max Lucado wrote a book titled <u>Just Like Jesus</u>. There is another ageless book titled <u>The Imitation of Christ</u>. I think, however, that for most of us a "sliver" of Christ is all we can ever hope to be. But just like in the parable of the mustard seed, a sliver of Christ can move mountains!

The Word of God

Gauge Yourself

"You don't have enough faith," Jesus told them. "I tell you the truth, if you had faith even as small as a mustard seed, you could say to this mountain, 'Move from here to there,' and it would move. Nothing would be impossible."

Matthew 17:20

Jesus sat down opposite the place where the offerings were put and watched the crowd putting their money into the temple treasury. Many rich people threw in large amounts. But a poor widow came and put in two very small copper coins, worth only a fraction of a penny.

Calling his disciples to him, Jesus said, "I tell you the truth, this poor widow has put more into the treasury than all the others. They all gave out of their wealth; but she, out of her poverty, put in everything—all she had to live on."

Mark 12:41-44

Prayer

Time to Refuel!

LORD, sometimes I feel awkward in giving because what I give is relatively small. I pray for a charitable heart and trust that what I do give, given humbly, will bear much fruit.

Life's Odometer

The distance we have traveled in life
Whether one year or one hundred
Cannot be changed or altered
No matter how much we have blundered

We have been where we have been
We have done what we have done
None of that can ever be changed
No matter what we've lost or what we've won

But in Christ we have a rare opportunity
To be renewed, to be "born again"
To start fresh, to start over
No matter our past, no matter our pain

In Christ, we can reset life's odometer
And head in a whole new direction
Renewed in mind, body, and soul
In Him we become a new creation

* * *

Reflection

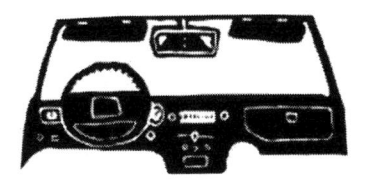

Looking Back – Moving Forward

It is human nature to dwell on the past. We cannot help but hit the playback button of our minds and watch our own lives like they were TV reruns. But inadvertently we sometimes trigger some of the same negative behavior, merely by focusing on it. It is a strange thing, but, if you think about it you will see it is true. In other words, thinking too much about our past sins sometimes keeps us trapped in them and makes it very difficult to move on. In Christ we find the strength to move forward, beyond past negative and sometimes destructive behavior.

The Word of God

Gauge Yourself

But when the kindness and love of God appeared, he saved us, not because of righteous things we had done, but because of his mercy. He saved us through the washing of rebirth and renewal by the Holy Spirit, whom he poured out on us generously through Jesus Christ our Savior, so that, having been justified by his grace, we might become heirs having the hope of eternal life.

Titus 3:4-7

Those who are dominated by the sinful nature think about sinful things, but those who are controlled by the Holy Spirit think about things that please the Spirit. So letting your sinful nature control your mind leads to death. But letting the Spirit control your mind leads to life and peace.

Romans 8:5-6

Prayer

Time to Refuel!

LORD, help me to get beyond my past sins and to move on with a renewed mind, one that is guided by the Holy Spirit, one that focuses on things above. Help me to stop watching reruns of my past negative behavior, but instead start living a life that is pleasing to you, one that is worthy of playback in heaven.

Holiness, the Final Frontier

Man has searched high, and man has searched low
Man has gone east, and man has gone west
In search of new territories, new lands to explore
From the beginning, this has been man's quest

Man, El Conquistador, continues in hot pursuit
To conquer and know all there is to know
With powerful microscopes and massive telescopes
Man's appetite for knowledge continues to grow

But with all that man has accomplished to date
There is still one last journey, one last frontier
A territory that to a large extent is still unexplored
A frontier that seems so far and yet is quite near

Holiness is that final frontier, virgin land if you will
Only a few in history have ever pierced its veil
And none have completely beheld it, owned it
But the One from above with each hand pierced by a nail

The final frontier is not space or the ocean floor
Its coast cannot be reached by spaceship or submarine
No telescope or microscope can capture its image
No scientist will yell "Eureka! I've discovered the gene"

Holiness, the final frontier, awaits us all
It's a journey each of us should undertake
And although we may struggle and falter along the way
It is the one frontier with the most at stake

And although we may struggle and falter along the way
It is the one frontier with the most at stake

* * *

Reflection

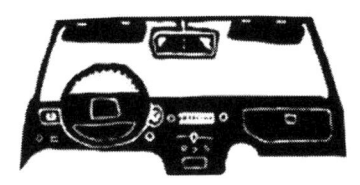

Looking Back – Moving Forward

Humans are very curious creatures. We are by nature explorers from birth. Over the centuries many explorers have died while attempting to reach new heights. But there is still so much to be accomplished not far from home, in our very own hearts and minds. Perhaps it is time to turn that ship around, make that final U-turn, and head to that final frontier – holiness – right here, right now.

The Word of God

Gauge Yourself

You were taught, with regard to your former way of life, to put off your old self, which is being corrupted by its deceitful desires; to be made new in the attitude of your minds; and to put on the new self, created to be like God in true righteousness and holiness.

Ephesians 4:22-24

Since we have these promises, dear friends, let us purify ourselves from everything that contaminates body and spirit, perfecting holiness out of reverence for God.

2 Corinthians 7:1

Make every effort to live in peace with all men and to be holy; without holiness no one will see the Lord.

Hebrews 12:14

Prayer

Time to Refuel!

LORD, I pray for renewal, rebirth, and holiness in my life. I know that holiness comes with much discipline, obedience, and sacrifice. But there is so much at stake! So, please help me turn this life around and get it moving in the right direction – towards you – for you are holy.

The Finish Line - <u>Not</u> the End!

At the 21st Winter Olympics in Vancouver, speed skater Sven Kramer of the Netherlands had a "lock" on a second gold medal but was disqualified because his coach mistakenly sent him into the wrong lane. It was a disastrous mistake for the Dutch skater. Afterwards, Kramer, visibly upset, conceded that ultimately lane changes are the skater's decision. That mistake cost Kramer a second gold medal.

There are several verses in the Bible about running a race. For example, *2 Timothy 4:7*: "I have fought the good fight, I have finished the race, I have kept the faith." Also, *1 Corinthians 9:24*: "Do you not know that in a race all the runners run, but only one gets the prize? Run in such a way as to get the prize." But the one verse that really gets my attention is *Galatians 5:7*: "You were running a good race. Who cut in on you and kept you from obeying the truth?"

Who cut in on you and kept you from obeying the truth? That is a very important question! When we find ourselves on the wrong path, how did we get there? When we find ourselves at a dead end, what exactly was it that got us there? When we come to a fork in the road, how is it that we decide which way to go – whose voice are we listening to? And when we find ourselves running a good race, staying faithful, and focused on the ultimate prize, who or what kept us from staying the course?

I struggle with these questions, as I am sure you do. It goes without saying that being a Christian does not immunize us from pain, suffering, bad decisions, bad habits, addictions, accidents, illnesses, and, of course, temptations. In fact, some of these things may loom even larger precisely because we are Christians, for example temptations and long-suffering. But the Bible gives us direction along that road. When we are lost, when someone cuts in on us and tries to lead us astray, we need to refocus, clean the crud (remember the scene from *My Cousin Vinny?*) that keeps us from seeing Christ clearly, and get back to running the good race.

In closing, "let us throw off everything that hinders and the sin that so easily entangles, and let us run with perseverance the race marked out for us." (*Hebrews 12:1*) Read and meditate upon this scripture, especially when you believe that someone or something has cut in on your race. If you find yourself so far off course that you need to do more than simply run faster, it is then that God, sometimes in a still small voice and other times quite forcefully, tells you that what you need to do is make a U-turn back to Him.

NOTES

Made in the USA
Charleston, SC
04 March 2011